contents

ingredients from a vietnamese kitchen	2
recipes	4
conversion chart	62
index	63

NZ, Canada, US and UK readers
Please note that Australian cup and spoon measurements are metric.
A conversion chart appears on page 62.

ingredients from a vietnamese kitchen

bamboo shoots

buk choy

galangal

sambal oelek

bamboo shoots tender, pale yellow, edible first-growth of the bamboo plant. Available fresh in Asian greengrocers, in season, but usually purchased canned; drain and rinse before use.
bean sprouts also known as bean shoots; tender new growths of assorted beans and seeds germinated for consumption as sprouts.
buk choy also known as bok choy, pak choi, chinese white cabbage or chinese chard; has a fresh, mild mustard taste.
chilli always use rubber gloves when seeding and chopping fresh chillies as they can burn your skin.
  long red available both fresh and dried; a generic term used for any moderately hot, long, thin chilli.
  powder the Asian variety is the hottest, made from dried ground thai chillies.
  thai also known as "scuds"; tiny, very hot and bright red in colour.
chinese barbecue duck traditionally cooked in special ovens, this duck has a sweet-sticky coating made from soy sauce, five-spice, sherry and hoisin sauce. Available from Asian grocery stores.
coriander also known as cilantro, pak chee or chinese parsley; bright-green-leafed herb having both pungent aroma and taste. Both the stems and roots of coriander are used in Vietnamese cooking: wash well before chopping.
fish sauce also called naam pla or nuoc naam. Made from pulverised salted fermented fish (most often anchovies); has a pungent smell and strong taste; use according to your taste.

five-spice powder a fragrant mixture of ground cinnamon, cloves, star anise, sichuan pepper and fennel seeds. Also known as chinese five-spice.
fried bean curd packaged pieces of deep-fried soft bean curd; the surface is brown and crunchy and the inside almost totally dried out.
fried shallots served as a condiment or sprinkled over just-cooked food, to add an extra crunchy finish. They can be purchased at Asian grocery stores; once opened, they will keep for months if stored in a tightly sealed glass jar.
gai lan also known as gai larn, chinese broccoli and chinese kale; a green vegetable appreciated more for its stems than its coarse leaves.
galangal also known as ka or lengkaus if fresh and laos if dried and powdered; a root similar to ginger in its use; has a hot, sour ginger-citrusy flavour.
ginger also known as green or root ginger; the thick gnarled root of a tropical plant. Ground or powdered ginger cannot be substituted for fresh.
hoisin sauce a thick, sweet and spicy chinese barbecue sauce made from salted fermented soybeans, onions and garlic; available from Asian food shops and supermarkets.
kecap manis also known as ketjap manis; a dark, thick sweet soy sauce with added sugar and spices.
lemon grass a tall, clumping, lemon-smelling and tasting, sharp-edged aromatic tropical grass; the white lower part of the stem is used, finely chopped.
mizuna frizzy green salad leaves with a delicate mustard flavour.

tamarind concentrate

vietnamese mint

palm sugar

star anise

lemon grass

noodles

  bean thread known as wun sen or cellophane or glass noodles because they become transparent when cooked.

  dried rice also known as rice stick noodles. Available flat and wide or very thin.

  fresh rice purchased in strands of various widths or large sheets weighing about 500g which are cut into the desired size.

  hokkien also known as stir-fry noodles; fresh wheat noodles resembling thick, yellow-brown spaghetti needing no pre-cooking before use.

  rice vermicelli also known as sen mee, mei fun or bee hoon; similar to bean thread noodles.

  singapore pre-cooked wheat noodles; a thinner version of hokkien.

oyster sauce a rich, brown sauce made from oysters and their brine, cooked with salt and soy sauce, and thickened with starches.

palm sugar made from the sap of the sugar palm tree. Light brown to black in colour; usually sold in rock-hard cakes. Substitute brown sugar for palm sugar, if unavailable.

rice paper sheets also known as banh trang. Made from rice paste and stamped into rounds; dipped in water they become pliable wrappers for fried food and uncooked vegetables.

rice wine vinegar made from fermented rice with no additives.

sambal oelek also ulek or olek; is a salty paste made from ground chillies and vinegar.

shiitake mushroom when dried is also known as donko or dried chinese mushrooms.

spring roll wrappers see *wonton wrappers*.

star anise a dried star-shaped pod whose seeds have an astringent aniseed flavour.

tamarind concentrate (or paste) a thick, purple-black, ready-to-use sweet-sour paste made from the pulp of tamarind tree pods; is available from most supermarkets and Asian food stores.

thai basil also known as horapa; has small leaves and purplish stems with a slight aniseed taste.

tofu also known as soybean curd or bean curd; an off-white, custard-like product made from the "milk" of crushed soybeans.

turmeric also known as kamin; is a rhizome related to galangal and ginger. Must be pounded to release its somewhat acrid aroma and pungent flavour.

vietnamese mint not a mint at all, but a pungent and peppery narrow-leafed member of the buckwheat family.

wombok also known as chinese cabbage, peking or napa cabbage; elongated in shape with pale green, crinkly leaves.

wonton wrappers and gow gee or spring roll wrappers, made of flour, egg and water, are found in the refrigerated or freezer section of Asian food shops and many supermarkets. These come in different thicknesses and shapes. Thin wrappers work best in soups, while the thicker ones are best for frying; and the choice of round or square, small or large is dependent on the recipe.

beef pho

Large bowls of pho (pronounced "fah") are a breakfast favourite throughout Vietnam, but we like to eat it any time of day.

3 litres (12 cups) water
1kg gravy beef
1 star anise
2.5cm piece (45g) fresh galangal
¼ cup (60ml) soy sauce
250g bean thread noodles
1¼ cups (100g) bean sprouts
¼ cup loosely packed fresh coriander leaves
⅓ cup loosely packed fresh vietnamese mint leaves
4 green onions, sliced thinly
1 fresh long red chilli, sliced thinly
⅓ cup (80ml) lime juice

1 Combine the water, beef, star anise, galangal and sauce in large saucepan; bring to a boil. Reduce heat; simmer, covered, 30 minutes. Uncover; simmer, 30 minutes or until beef is tender.
2 Place noodles in medium heatproof bowl, cover with boiling water; stand until just tender, drain.
3 Combine remaining ingredients in medium bowl.
4 Remove beef from pan; reserve broth. Remove fat and sinew from beef; slice thinly. Return beef to pan; reheat until broth just comes to a boil.
5 Divide noodles among serving bowls; top with hot beef and broth then sprout mixture.

serves 6
preparation time 10 minutes
cooking time 1 hour 15 minutes
per serving 9.9g total fat (4.2g saturated fat); 1212kJ (290 cal); 12g carbohydrate; 36.7g protein; 1.6g fibre
tip Round, skirt or chuck steak are all suitable for this recipe. Gravy beef is also known as shin beef.

chicken pho

3 litres (12 cups) chicken stock
12cm piece fresh ginger (60g), sliced thinly
2 tablespoons fish sauce
2 cloves garlic, quartered
½ cup coarsely chopped fresh coriander root and stem mixture
1 star anise
340g chicken breast fillets, sliced thinly
400g dried rice noodles
12 green onions, sliced
3 cups (240g) bean sprouts
½ cup loosely packed fresh vietnamese mint leaves
½ cup loosely packed fresh coriander leaves
1 medium lemon (140g), cut into wedges
sambal oelek, to serve

1 Combine stock, ginger, sauce, garlic, coriander root and stem mixture and star anise in large saucepan; bring to a boil. Reduce heat; simmer, uncovered, 10 minutes. Strain stock into large heatproof jug; discard solids.
2 Return stock to pan, add chicken; simmer, uncovered, about 5 minutes or until chicken is cooked.
3 Place noodles in medium heatproof bowl, cover with boiling water; stand until just tender, drain.
4 Divide noodles, onion and sprouts among serving bowls; pour over hot soup, top with mint and coriander leaves. Serve with lemon wedges and sambal oelek.

serves 6
preparation time 20 minutes
cooking time 30 minutes
per serving 3.8g total fat (1.4g saturated fat); 890kJ (213 cal); 20.7g carbohydrate; 22.2g protein; 3g fibre
tip You need 1 bunch of fresh coriander with stems and roots intact for this recipe; wash well before chopping.

chicken wonton soup

2kg chicken bones
2 medium brown onions (300g), chopped coarsely
2 trimmed celery stalks (200g), chopped coarsely
2 medium carrots (240g), chopped coarsely
3 bay leaves
2 teaspoons black peppercorns
5 litres (20 cups) water
2 tablespoons dark soy sauce
1 clove garlic, crushed
1cm piece fresh ginger (5g), grated
500g baby buk choy, chopped coarsely
2 green onions, sliced thinly

chicken wontons
300g chicken mince
1 tablespoon dark soy sauce
1 clove garlic, crushed
1 teaspoon sesame oil
4 green onions, chopped finely
40 wonton wrappers

1 Combine bones, brown onion, celery, carrot, bay leaves, peppercorns and the water in large saucepan; bring to a boil. Reduce heat; simmer, uncovered, 2 hours, skimming occasionally.
2 Strain stock through muslin-lined strainer into large bowl; discard solids. Cover stock; refrigerate 3 hours or overnight.
3 Make chicken wontons.
4 Remove and discard fat from surface of stock. Return stock to large saucepan with sauce, garlic and ginger. Bring to a boil.
5 Add chicken wontons; simmer, uncovered, about 5 minutes or until wontons float to the surface. Just before serving, stir remaining ingredients into soup.

chicken wontons Combine mince, sauce, garlic, oil and onion in medium bowl. Brush edge of each wonton wrapper with water. Place a rounded teaspoon of chicken mixture in centre of wrapper; pinch edges together to seal. Repeat with remaining wrappers and chicken mixture.

serves 8
preparation time 20 minutes (plus refrigeration time)
cooking time 2 hours 10 minutes
per serving 2.9g total fat (0.7g saturated fat); 836kJ (200 cal); 27.5g carbohydrate; 14.2g protein; 2.7g fibre
tip Stock and wontons can be made in advance and frozen, separately.

prawn soup

500g uncooked king prawns
2cm piece fresh ginger (10g), sliced thinly
1 teaspoon black peppercorns
2 cloves garlic, crushed
10cm stick fresh lemon grass (20g), chopped finely
3 litres (12 cups) water
2 large fresh red chillies, sliced thinly
400g fresh rice noodles
¼ cup (60ml) lemon juice
⅓ cup (80ml) fish sauce, approximately
2 green onions, sliced thinly
⅓ cup firmly packed fresh coriander leaves
¼ cup firmly packed fresh mint leaves

1 Peel and devein prawns, discard heads. Place prawn shells, ginger, peppercorns, garlic, lemon grass, the water and half the chilli in large saucepan; bring to a boil. Reduce heat; simmer, uncovered, 20 minutes. Strain stock, discard solids; return liquid to cleaned pan.
2 Add prawns to stock; simmer, covered, about 3 minutes or until prawns are changed in colour.
3 Place noodles in medium heatproof bowl, cover with boiling water; stand until just tender, drain.
4 Add juice to stock, gradually add sauce to taste.
5 Divide prawns and noodles among serving bowls; top with stock, onion, herbs and remaining chilli.

serves 6
preparation time 30 minutes
cooking time 25 minutes
per serving 0.7g total fat (0g saturated fat); 497kJ (119 cal); 15.8g carbohydrate; 11.3g protein; 1.1g fibre

steamed sesame scallops

1½ cups (300g) jasmine rice
20 scallops, roe removed (500g) on the half shell
3cm piece fresh ginger (15g), cut into matchsticks
10cm stick fresh lemon grass (20g) chopped finely
4 green onions, sliced thinly
1 tablespoon sesame oil
¼ cup (60ml) kecap manis
¼ cup (60ml) soy sauce

1 Cook rice in large saucepan of boiling water, uncovered, until just tender; drain.
2 Place scallops, in batches, in single layer in large bamboo steamer; top with ginger, lemon grass and onion. Cover; steam scallops about 5 minutes or until tender and cooked.
3 Divide scallops among serving plates; top with combined remaining ingredients. Serve with rice.

serves 4
preparation time 15 minutes
cooking time 15 minutes
per serving 5.5g total fat (0.9g saturated fat); 1522kJ (364 cal); 61.2g carbohydrate; 15.6g protein; 0.9g fibre

salt and lemon-pepper squid

600g squid hoods
½ cup (75g) plain flour
2 teaspoons coarse cooking salt
1 tablespoon lemon pepper
peanut oil, for deep-frying

1 Halve squid hoods lengthways, score insides in crosshatch pattern; cut each half lengthways into five pieces. Toss squid in medium bowl with combined flour, salt and lemon pepper until coated; shake off excess.
2 Heat oil in wok; deep-fry squid, in batches, until tender and browned lightly. Drain.
3 Serve squid with spicy dipping sauce (page 60), if desired.

serves 4
preparation time 15 minutes
cooking time 15 minutes
per serving 10.3g total fat (2.1g saturated fat); 1053kJ (252 cal); 12.6g carbohydrate; 26.9g protein; 0.7g fibre

spring rolls

1 medium red capsicum (200g)
1 tablespoon peanut oil
700g chicken breast fillets
4cm piece fresh ginger (20g), grated
2 cloves garlic, crushed
4 green onions, chopped finely
100g bean thread noodles
1 medium carrot (120g), cut into matchsticks
1 tablespoon coarsely chopped fresh vietnamese mint
500g buk choy, sliced finely
¼ cup (60ml) sweet chilli sauce
1 tablespoon soy sauce
40 spring roll wrappers
peanut oil, for deep-frying

1 Halve capsicum, discard seeds and membrane; slice into very thin strips.
2 Heat half the oil in medium saucepan; cook chicken, in batches, until browned and cooked. Cool 10 minutes; shred finely.
3 Heat remaining oil in same pan; cook ginger, garlic and onion, stirring, about 2 minutes or until onion is soft.
4 Meanwhile, place noodles in medium heatproof bowl, cover with boiling water; stand until just tender, drain. Chop noodles coarsely.
5 Combine capsicum, carrot, chicken, onion mixture and noodles in large bowl with mint, buk choy and sauces.
6 Place a rounded tablespoon of the mixture across edge of one wrapper; roll to enclose filling, folding in ends. Place on tray, seam-side down. Repeat with remaining mixture and wrappers; place on tray in single layer.
7 Heat oil in wok; deep-fry spring rolls, in batches, until golden brown and cooked through; drain on absorbent paper.
8 Serve spring rolls with sweet chilli dipping sauce (page 60), if desired.

makes 40
preparation time 1 hour
cooking time 25 minutes
per roll 3.8g total fat (0.7g saturated fat); 305kJ (73 cal); 4.6g carbohydrate; 4.8g protein; 0.6g fibre
tips Freeze spring rolls, in single layer, between sheets of plastic wrap. This makes it easier to remove small quantities at a time. Frozen spring rolls can be deep-fried.

coconut chicken summer rolls

300g chicken tenderloins
½ cup (125ml) coconut cream
½ cup (125ml) chicken stock
10cm stick fresh lemon grass (20g), chopped coarsely
5cm piece fresh ginger (25g), grated
1 tablespoon coarsely chopped fresh coriander root and stem mixture
100g snow peas, trimmed, sliced thinly
½ cup coarsely chopped fresh coriander
12 x 17cm-square rice paper sheets

1 Combine chicken, coconut cream, stock, lemon grass, ginger and coriander root and stem mixture in medium saucepan; bring to a boil. Reduce heat; simmer, uncovered, about 5 minutes or until chicken is cooked. Cool chicken in poaching liquid 10 minutes. Remove chicken from pan; reserve ¼ cup of the poaching liquid, discard remainder.
2 Chop chicken finely; place in medium bowl with snow peas, coriander and poaching liquid, toss gently to combine.
3 To assemble rolls, place 1 sheet of rice paper in medium bowl of warm water until just softened. Carefully lift sheet from water; place, with one point facing you, on board covered with tea towel. Place a little of the chicken filling vertically along centre of sheet; fold top and bottom corners over filling then roll sheet from side to side to enclose filling. Repeat with remaining rice paper sheets and chicken filling.
4 Serve rolls with sweet chilli dipping sauce (page 60), if desired.

makes 12
preparation time 20 minutes
cooking time 10 minutes
per roll 3.4g total fat (2.2g saturated fat); 305kJ (73 cal); 4g carbohydrate; 6.3g protein; 0.6g fibre
tip You will need 1 bunch of fresh coriander with stems and roots intact for this recipe; wash well before chopping.

noodle and vegetable summer rolls

60g rice vermicelli
½ medium carrot (60g), grated coarsely
½ small wombok (350g), shredded finely
1 tablespoon fish sauce
1 tablespoon brown sugar
¼ cup (60ml) lemon juice
12 x 17cm-square rice paper sheets
12 large fresh mint leaves

1 Place vermicelli in medium heatproof bowl, cover with boiling water; stand until just tender, drain. Cut into random lengths.
2 Place vermicelli in medium bowl with carrot, wombok, sauce, sugar and juice; toss gently to combine.
3 To assemble rolls, place 1 sheet of rice paper in medium bowl of warm water until just softened. Carefully lift sheet from water; place, with one point facing you, on board covered with tea towel. Place a little of the vegetable filling and one mint leaf vertically along centre of sheet; fold top and bottom corners over filling then roll sheet from side to side to enclose filling. Repeat with remaining rice paper sheets, vegetable filling and mint leaves.
4 Serve rolls with sweet chilli dipping sauce (page 60), if desired.

makes 12
preparation time 20 minutes
cooking time 5 minutes
per roll 0.2g total fat (0g saturated fat); 167kJ (40 cal); 7.6g carbohydrate; 1.4g protein; 0.8g fibre

pork and prawn summer rolls

200g pork belly
650g cooked medium king prawns
1⅓ cups (80g) finely shredded iceberg lettuce
1 cup (80g) bean sprouts
½ cup loosely packed fresh mint leaves
12 x 17cm-square rice paper sheets

1 Cover pork with water in medium saucepan, cover; bring to a boil. Reduce heat; simmer, uncovered, about 45 minutes or until pork is tender. Drain; when cool enough to handle, slice thinly.
2 Shell and devein prawns; chop prawn meat finely.
3 Combine lettuce, sprouts and mint in medium bowl.
4 To assemble rolls, place 1 sheet of rice paper in medium bowl of warm water until just softened. Carefully lift sheet from water; place, with one point facing you, on board covered with tea towel. Place a little of the prawn meat vertically along centre of sheet; top with a little of the pork then a little of the lettuce filling. Fold top and bottom corners over filling then roll sheet from side to side to enclose filling. Repeat with remaining rice paper sheets, prawn meat, pork and lettuce filling.
5 Serve rolls with hoisin and peanut dipping sauce (page 61), if desired.

makes 12
preparation time 35 minutes
cooking time 50 minutes
per roll 3.5g total fat (1.2g saturated fat); 347kJ (83 cal); 3.3g carbohydrate; 9g protein; 0.6g fibre

barbecued chilli prawns with fresh mango salad

1kg uncooked large king prawns
½ teaspoon ground turmeric
1 teaspoon chilli powder
2 teaspoons sweet paprika
2 cloves garlic, crushed

fresh mango salad
2 large mangoes (1.2kg), chopped coarsely
1 small red onion (100g), sliced thinly
1 fresh long red chilli, sliced thinly
1½ cups (120g) bean sprouts
½ cup coarsely chopped fresh coriander
2 teaspoons fish sauce
2 teaspoons grated palm sugar
2 tablespoons lime juice
1 tablespoon peanut oil

1 Make mango salad.
2 Shell and devein prawns, leaving tails intact. Combine turmeric, chilli, paprika and garlic in large bowl; add prawns, toss prawns to coat in mixture.
3 Cook prawns, in batches, on heated oiled grill plate (or grill or barbecue) until browned lightly. Serve prawns with mango salad.
fresh mango salad Place ingredients in medium bowl; toss gently.

serves 4
preparation time 25 minutes
cooking time 10 minutes
per serving 5.9g total fat (1g saturated fat); 1279kJ (306 cal); 30.8g carbohydrate; 29.6g protein; 4.9g fibre

chicken salad

500g chicken breast fillets
1 large carrot (180g),
  cut into matchsticks
½ cup (125ml) rice wine vinegar
2 teaspoons salt
2 tablespoons caster sugar
1 medium white onion (150g),
  sliced thinly
1½ cups (120g) bean sprouts
2 cups (160g) finely shredded
  savoy cabbage
¼ cup firmly packed fresh
  vietnamese mint leaves
½ cup firmly packed fresh
  coriander leaves
1 tablespoon crushed
  roasted peanuts
2 tablespoons fried shallots

dressing
2 tablespoons fish sauce
¼ cup (60ml) water
2 tablespoons caster sugar
2 tablespoons lime juice
1 clove garlic, crushed

1 Place chicken in medium saucepan of boiling water; return to a boil. Reduce heat; simmer, uncovered, about 10 minutes or until cooked. Cool chicken in poaching liquid 10 minutes; discard liquid. Shred chicken coarsely.
2 Make dressing.
3 Combine carrot in large bowl with vinegar, salt and sugar; cover, stand 5 minutes. Add onion; cover, stand 5 minutes. Add sprouts; cover, stand 3 minutes. Drain pickled vegetables; discard liquid.
4 Place pickled vegetables in large bowl with chicken, cabbage, mint and coriander.
5 Pour dressing over salad; toss gently to combine. Sprinkle with nuts and shallots.
dressing Combine ingredients in screw-top jar; shake well.

serves 4
preparation time 20 minutes
cooking time 15 minutes
per serving 4.6g total fat (1g saturated fat); 1191kJ (295 cal); 25.3g carbohydrate; 32.6g protein; 4.6g fibre

duck salad

1kg chinese barbecued duck
150g snow peas, trimmed, sliced thinly
1 green mango (350g), sliced thinly
3 shallots (75g), sliced thinly
125g mizuna
⅓ cup firmly packed fresh mint leaves
⅓ cup firmly packed fresh coriander leaves
1 fresh long red chilli, sliced thinly
dressing
2 tablespoons fish sauce
2 tablespoons grated palm sugar
⅓ cup (80ml) lime juice
2 teaspoons peanut oil

1 Make dressing.
2 Remove meat from duck, leaving skin; discard bones. Chop meat coarsely; place in large bowl with remaining ingredients.
3 Pour dressing over salad; toss gently.
dressing Combine ingredients in screw-top jar; shake well.

serves 4
preparation time 25 minutes
per serving 39.8g total fat (11.5g saturated fat); 2337kJ (559 cal); 17.8g carbohydrate; 31.7g protein; 3.2g fibre

duck and noodle salad

2 medium carrots (240g), cut into matchsticks
150g snow peas, sliced thinly
150g baby corn, quartered lengthways
250g dried rice noodles
1kg chinese barbecued duck
1 cup (80g) bean sprouts
¼ cup coarsely chopped fresh vietnamese mint
¼ cup coarsely chopped fresh coriander
2 fresh small red thai chillies, chopped finely
ginger and lemon grass dressing
2cm piece fresh ginger (10g), grated
10cm stick fresh lemon grass (20g), chopped finely
2 tablespoons grated palm sugar
½ cup (125ml) lime juice
2 tablespoons fish sauce

1 Plunge carrot, snow peas and corn in large saucepan of boiling water 30 seconds; rinse immediately under cold water.
2 Place noodles in medium heatproof bowl; cover with boiling water, stand until just tender, drain.
3 Make ginger and lemon grass dressing.
4 Remove and discard skin and bones from duck; slice meat thinly.
5 Place vegetables, noodles and duck in large bowl with sprouts, herbs, chilli and dressing; toss gently to combine.

ginger and lemon grass dressing Combine ingredients in screw-top jar; shake well.

serves 4
preparation time 20 minutes
per serving 38.4g total fat (11.2g saturated fat); 2968kJ (710 cal); 51.9g carbohydrate; 36.1g protein; 5.8g fibre

hot-smoked trout and vermicelli salad

We used two hot-smoked ocean trout portions, weighing approximately 200g each. It can be found, cryovac-packed, in the refrigerated section of supermarkets and at fish shops. You can also use cold-smoked trout, if preferred.

200g rice vermicelli
400g hot-smoked trout fillets
2 trimmed celery stalks (200g), sliced thinly
2 lebanese cucumbers (260g), seeded, sliced thinly
½ cup (70g) roasted shelled pistachios
¼ cup coarsely chopped fresh mint
¼ cup coarsely chopped fresh thai basil

dressing
⅓ cup (80ml) lime juice
1 teaspoon chilli oil
1 tablespoon sesame oil
2 tablespoons fish sauce
1 clove garlic, crushed

1 Place vermicelli in medium heatproof bowl, cover with boiling water, stand until just tender; drain.
2 Make dressing.
3 Discard skin and bones from fish. Flake fish into large pieces in large bowl; add noodles, celery, cucumber, nuts and herbs.
4 Drizzle dressing over salad; toss gently.
dressing Combine ingredients in screw-top jar; shake well.

serves 4
preparation time 25 minutes
per serving 20.9g total fat (3.2g saturated fat); 1923kJ (460 cal); 32.4g carbohydrate; 32.9g protein; 4.1g fibre
tip Add more chilli oil to the dressing if you want to make the salad hotter, or use a finely chopped fresh chilli if chilli oil is unavailable.

pan-fried tofu with coleslaw salad

400g firm silken tofu
2 medium carrots (240g)
2 cups (160g) finely shredded green cabbage
2 cups (160g) finely shredded red cabbage
2 small yellow capsicum (300g), sliced thinly
2 cups (160g) bean sprouts
6 green onions, sliced thinly
1 cup loosely packed fresh coriander leaves
lime and garlic dressing
½ cup (125ml) lime juice
2 cloves garlic, crushed

1 Place tofu, in single layer, on absorbent-paper-lined tray; cover tofu with more absorbent paper, stand 10 minutes.
2 Meanwhile, using vegetable peeler, slice carrot into ribbons. Place in medium bowl with cabbages, capsicum, sprouts, onion and coriander; toss gently.
3 Cut tofu into four slices; cook tofu in heated lightly oiled small frying pan until browned both sides.
4 Make lime and garlic dressing.
5 Drizzle dressing over salad; serve with tofu.
lime and garlic dressing Combine ingredients in screw-top jar; shake well.

serves 4
preparation time 30 minutes
cooking time 5 minutes
per serving 7.3g total fat (1g saturated fat); 807kJ (193 cal); 9.9g carbohydrate; 16.9g protein; 9g fibre

prawn and vermicelli salad

60g rice vermicelli
400g cooked medium king prawns
2 green onions, sliced thinly
1 small red capsicum (150g), sliced thinly
1 small green capsicum (150g), sliced thinly
1 lebanese cucumber (130g), seeded, sliced thinly
2 tablespoons finely shredded fresh vietnamese mint
¼ cup loosely packed fresh coriander leaves
1 tablespoon fried shallots

dressing

1½ tablespoons fish sauce
1 tablespoon lime juice
1 tablespoon water
2 teaspoons brown sugar

1 Place vermicelli in large heatproof bowl, cover with boiling water; stand until just tender, drain. Cut into random lengths.
2 Make dressing.
3 Shell and devein prawns; halve prawns lengthways.
4 Place vermicelli, prawns, onion, capsicums, cucumber, herbs and dressing in large serving bowl; toss gently to combine. Top with shallots; serve immediately.
dressing Combine ingredients in screw-top jar; shake well.

serves 4
preparation time 20 minutes
cooking time 5 minutes
per serving 0.7g total fat (0.1g saturated fat); 477kJ (114 cal); 12.9g carbohydrate; 12.9g protein; 1.4g fibre

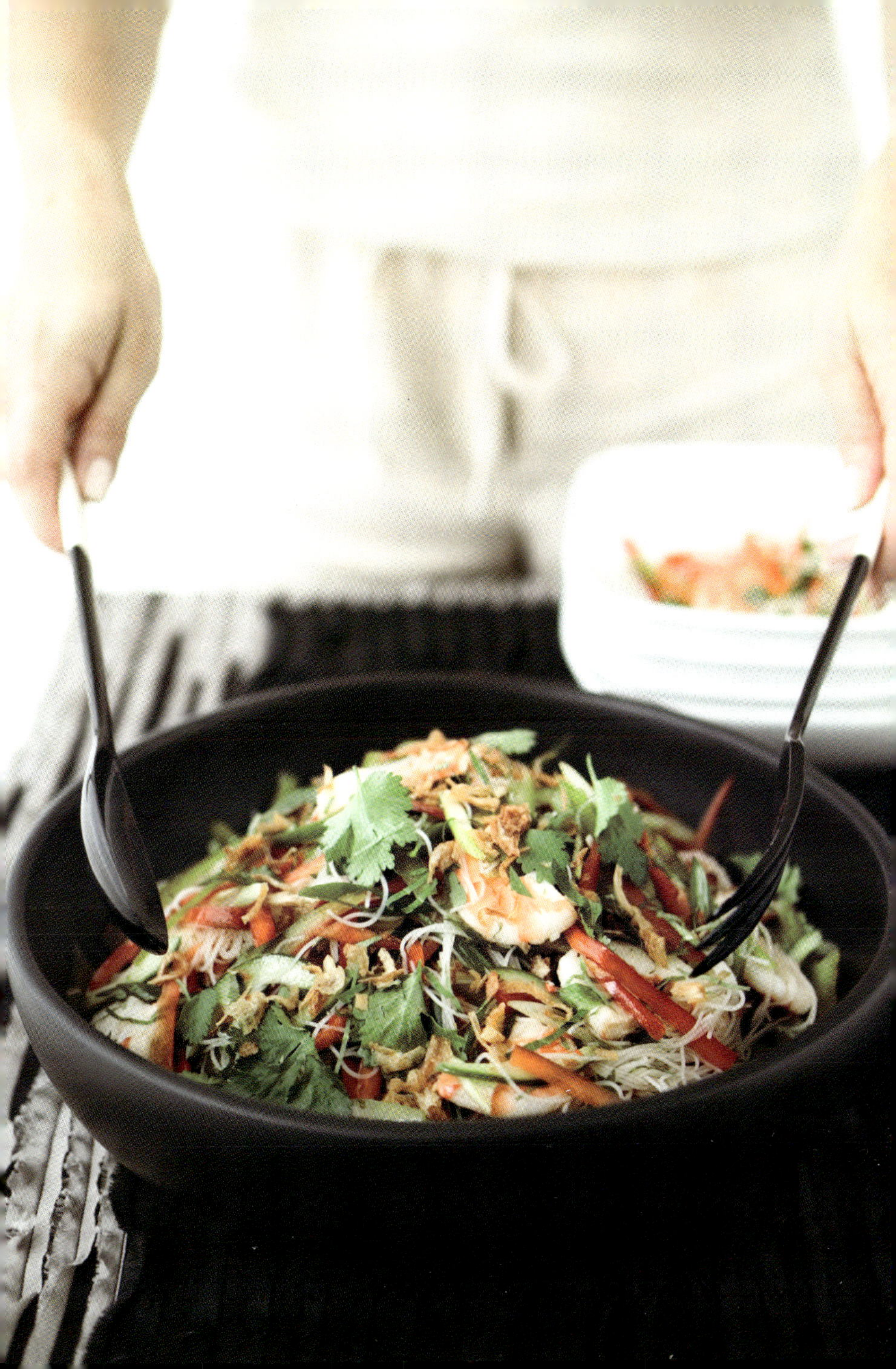

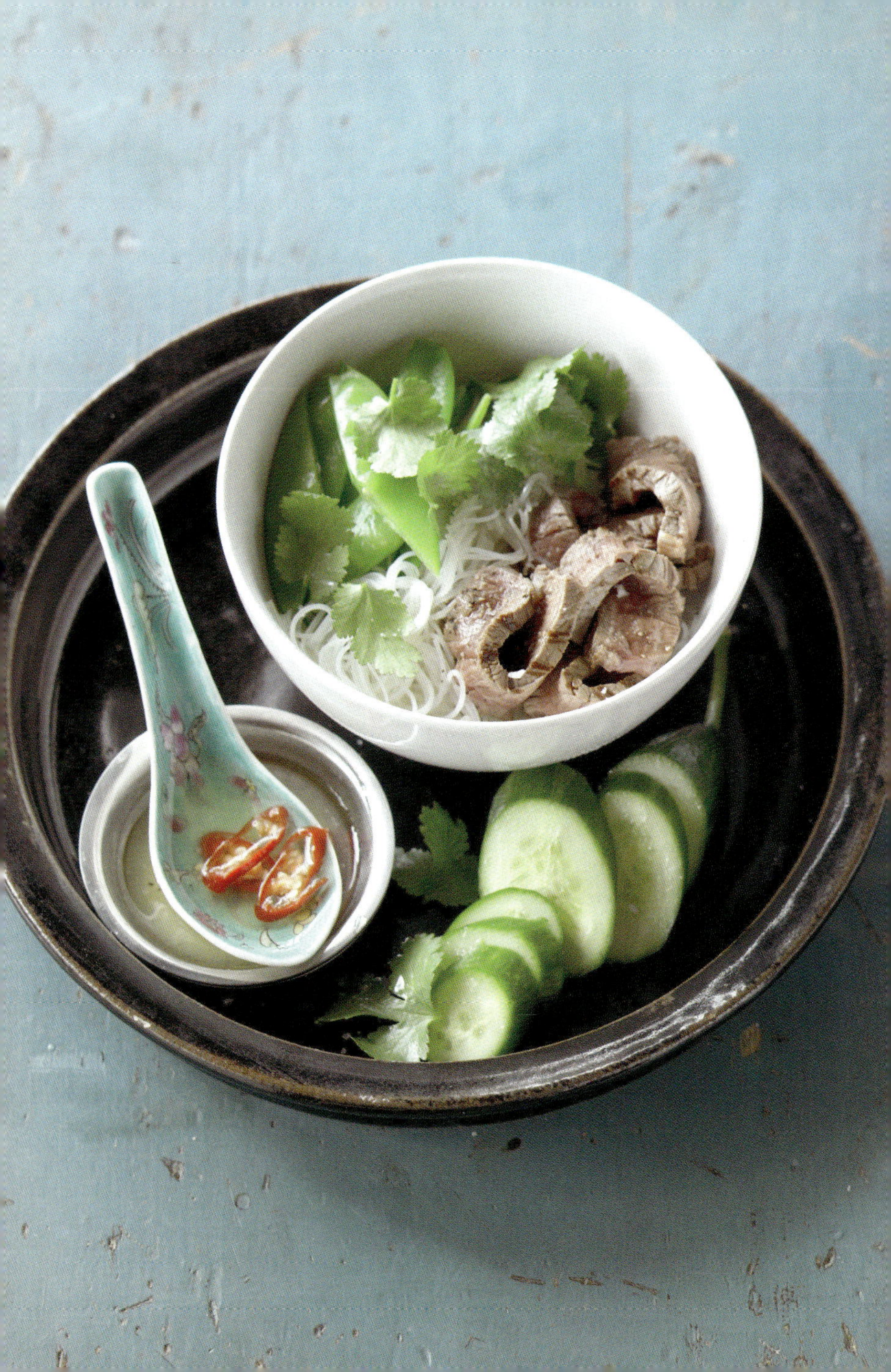

beef and rice noodle salad

400g beef rump steak
100g rice vermicelli
150g snow peas
2 lebanese cucumbers (260g), sliced thickly
⅓ cup fresh coriander leaves
lime and chilli dressing
¼ cup (60ml) lime juice
2 tablespoons peanut oil
1 fresh small red thai chilli, sliced thinly

1 Cook beef on heated oiled grill plate (or grill or barbecue) until browned both sides and cooked as desired. Cover, stand 5 minutes then slice thinly.
2 Place vermicelli in large heatproof bowl, cover with boiling water; stand until just tender, drain.
3 Cut snow peas in half diagonally.
4 Make lime and chilli dressing.
5 Combine beef, noodles, snow peas and cucumber in bowl with dressing; sprinkle with coriander.
lime and chilli dressing Combine ingredients in screw top jar; shake well.

serves 4
preparation time 10 minutes
cooking time 10 minutes
per serving 16.3g total fat (4.6g saturated fat); 1346kJ (322 cal); 17.3g carbohydrate; 25.4g protein; 1.7g fibre

vegetable omelettes

5 dried shiitake mushrooms
1 tablespoon peanut oil
5 green onions, sliced thinly
2 cloves garlic, crushed
230g can sliced bamboo shoots, drained
1 medium carrot (120g), sliced thinly
1 large red capsicum (350g), sliced thinly
1 cup (80g) bean sprouts
1 tablespoon mild chilli sauce
2 tablespoons light soy sauce
1 tablespoon finely chopped fresh coriander
8 eggs
½ cup (125ml) milk
1 tablespoon finely chopped vietnamese mint

1 Place mushrooms in small heatproof bowl; cover with boiling water. Stand 20 minutes; drain. Discard stems; slice caps thinly.
2 Heat half the oil in medium frying pan; cook onion, garlic and bamboo shoots, stirring, until onion softens. Add carrot and capsicum; cook, stirring, until carrot is just tender. Add mushrooms, sprouts, sauces and coriander; cook, stirring, until heated through. Remove from pan; keep warm.
3 Whisk eggs, milk and mint in medium bowl until combined.
4 Heat remaining oil in pan. Add a quarter of the egg mixture; cook over medium heat, tilting pan, until egg mixture is almost set. Place a quarter of the vegetable mixture evenly over half of the omelette. Fold omelette over to enclose filling; slide onto serving plate. Repeat process with remaining egg and vegetable mixtures.

serves 4
preparation time 10 minutes (plus standing time)
cooking time 15 minutes
per serving 16.7g total fat (4.9g saturated fat); 1120kJ (268 cal); 10.3g carbohydrate; 17.8g protein; 3.9g fibre

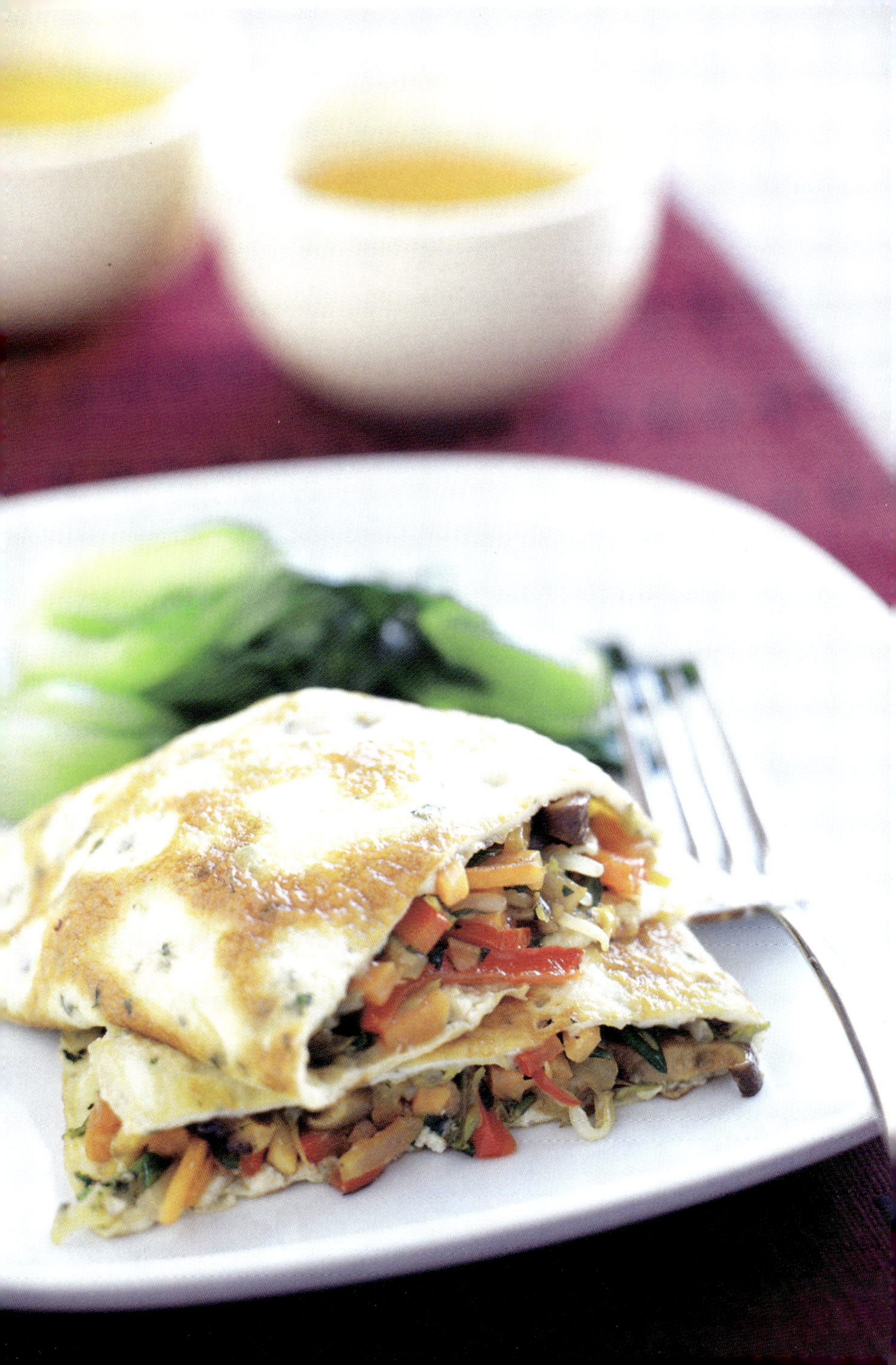

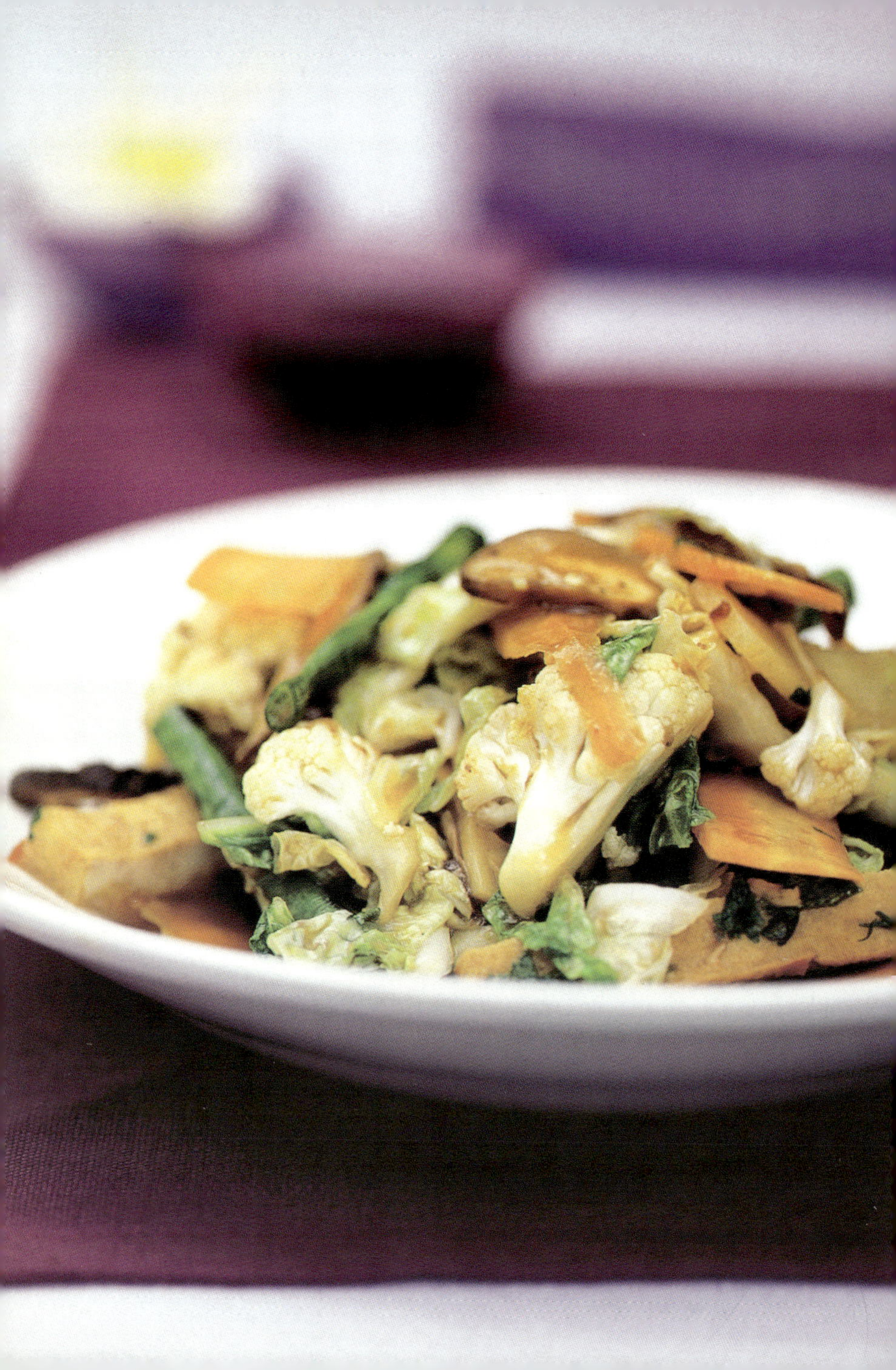

stir-fried mixed vegetables

190g fried tofu, cut into 1cm slices
⅓ cup (80ml) soy sauce
2 tablespoons coarsely chopped fresh coriander
1 teaspoon honey
6 dried shiitake mushrooms
1 tablespoon peanut oil
3 cloves garlic, crushed
2cm piece fresh ginger (10g), grated
10cm stick fresh lemon grass (20g), chopped finely
2 medium carrots (240g), cut into 6cm strips
200g snake beans, cut into 6cm lengths
500g cauliflower, cut into florets
230g can bamboo shoots, rinsed, drained
600g wombok, chopped coarsely
¾ cup (180ml) vegetable stock
1 tablespoon cornflour
2 teaspoons hoisin sauce
1 teaspoon lime juice
½ teaspoon sambal oelek

1 Combine tofu, soy sauce, coriander and honey in small bowl.
2 Place mushrooms in small heatproof bowl; cover with boiling water. Stand 20 minutes; drain. Discard stems; slice caps thinly.
3 Heat oil in wok; stir-fry garlic, ginger and lemon grass until fragrant. Add carrots, beans and cauliflower; stir-fry until vegetables are just tender.
4 Add tofu mixture to wok with bamboo shoots, mushrooms and wombok; stir-fry until heated through. Stir in blended stock, cornflour, hoisin sauce, juice and sambal oelek; stir over heat until mixture boils and thickens slightly.

serves 6
preparation time 15 minutes (plus standing time)
cooking time 10 minutes
per serving 5.8g total fat (1g saturated fat); 598kJ (143 cal); 10.2g carbohydrate; 9.4g protein; 6.3g fibre

prawn tamarind stir-fry with buk choy

1kg uncooked medium king prawns
2 tablespoons peanut oil
4 green onions, sliced thinly lengthways
4 cloves garlic, sliced thinly
1 teaspoon cornflour
½ cup (125ml) vegetable stock
2 tablespoons oyster sauce
1 tablespoon tamarind concentrate
1 teaspoon sambal oelek
2 teaspoons sesame oil
1 tablespoon lime juice
1 tablespoon brown sugar
350g yellow patty-pan squash, sliced thickly
300g sugar snap peas, trimmed
800g baby buk choy, chopped coarsely

1 Shell and devein prawns, leaving tails intact.

2 Heat half of the peanut oil in wok; stir-fry onion and garlic, separately, until browned lightly. Drain.

3 Blend cornflour and stock in small jug; stir in sauce, tamarind, sambal oelek, sesame oil, juice and sugar.

4 Heat remaining peanut oil in wok; stir-fry prawns, in batches, until changed in colour and almost cooked through. Add squash to wok; stir-fry until just tender. Add cornflour mixture; stir-fry until sauce boils and thickens slightly. Return prawns to wok with peas and buk choy; stir-fry until buk choy just wilts and prawns are cooked through.

5 Top stir-fry with reserved onion and garlic; serve with steamed jasmine rice, if desired.

serves 4
preparation time 25 minutes
cooking time 10 minutes
per serving 13.3g total fat (2.2g saturated fat); 1396kJ (334 cal);16.3g carbohydrate; 33.5g protein; 7.2g fibre

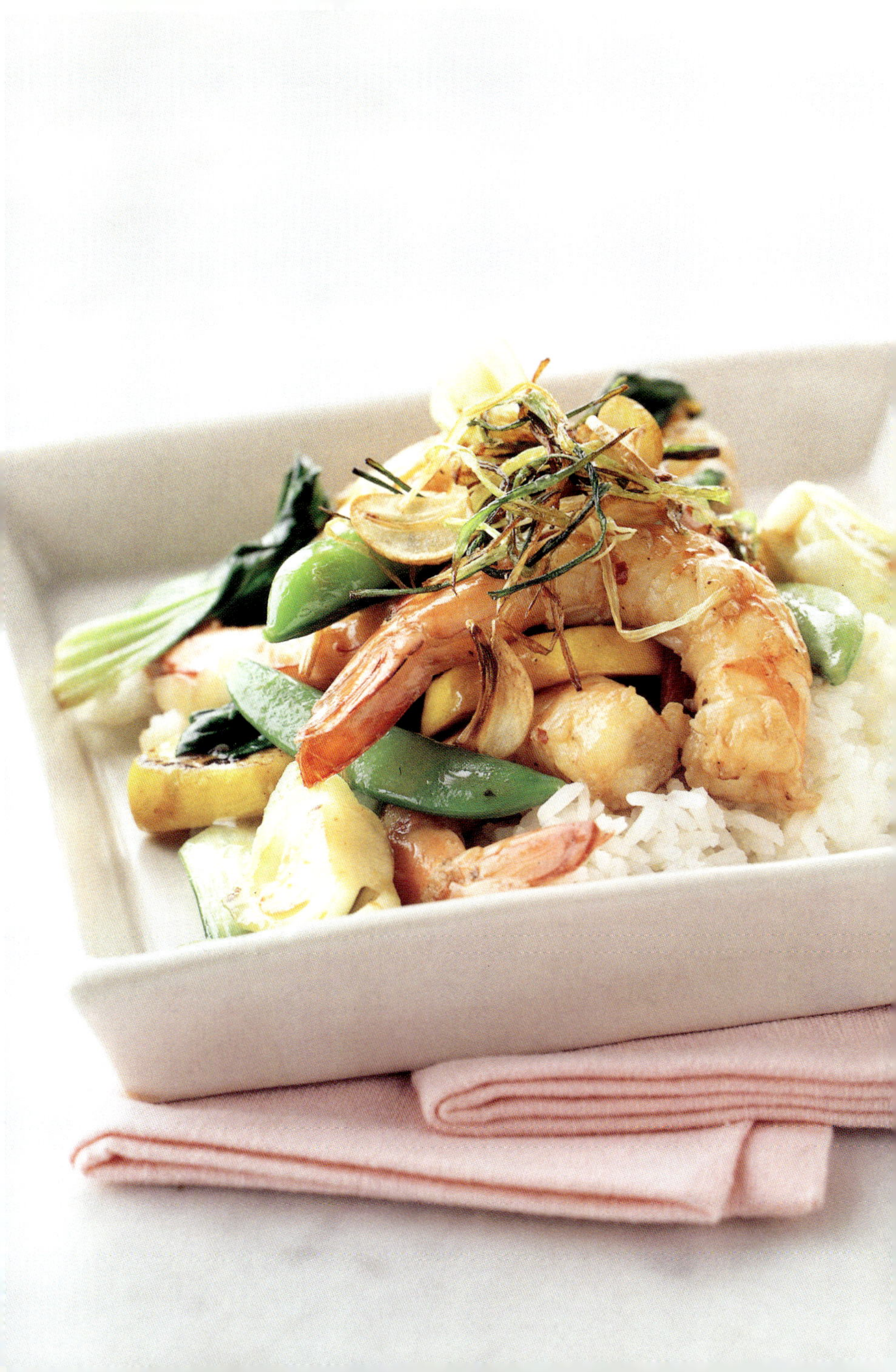

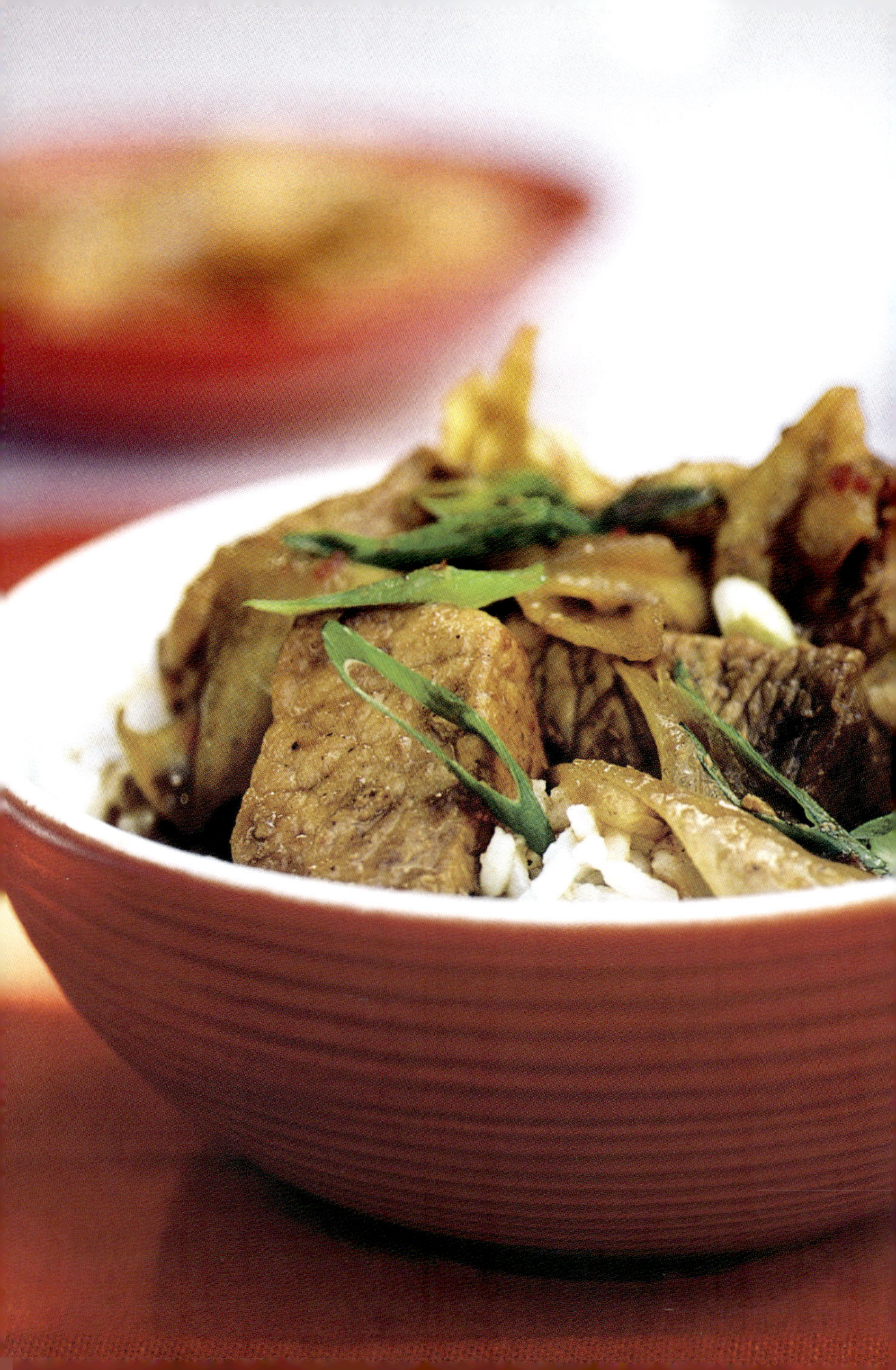

spiced caramel pork

1 tablespoon peanut oil
750g pork neck, cut into 3cm pieces
1 large brown onion (200g), cut into wedges
1 cup (250ml) water
⅓ cup (75g) white sugar
1 tablespoon fish sauce
½ teaspoon sambal oelek
¼ teaspoon five-spice powder
1 green onion, chopped finely

1 Heat oil in large frying pan; cook pork, stirring, until browned and tender. Add onion; cook, stirring, until onion is soft. Cover pan; remove from heat.
2 Combine ¼ cup (60ml) of the water with sugar in small saucepan; stir over heat, without boiling, until sugar dissolves. Boil, uncovered, without stirring, until sugar syrup is golden brown. Add the remaining water and sauce to sugar syrup; stir over low heat until smooth. Reduce heat; simmer, uncovered, until mixture reduced to about ½ cup (125ml).
3 Stir sauce mixture into pork in pan with sambal oelek and five-spice; simmer, uncovered, about 5 minutes or until pork is heated through.
4 Top pork with green onion; serve with steamed rice, if desired.

serves 4
preparation time 10 minutes
cooking time 35 minutes
per serving 7.7g total fat (1.8g saturated fat); 1413kJ (338 cal); 23.3g carbohydrate; 43.9g protein; 1.1g fibre

lemon grass and asparagus beef

500g piece beef fillet, sliced thinly
3 cloves garlic, crushed
10cm stick fresh lemon grass (20g), chopped finely
1 teaspoon brown sugar
1 teaspoon salt
2 tablespoons peanut oil
250g asparagus, halved
1 large brown onion (200g), cut into wedges
1cm piece fresh ginger (5g), grated
2 medium tomatoes (360g), cut into wedges
2 tablespoons coarsely chopped fresh coriander
2 tablespoons unsalted roasted peanuts

1 Combine beef, garlic, lemon grass, sugar, salt and half the oil in large bowl. Cover; refrigerate 3 hours or overnight.
2 Boil, steam or microwave asparagus until just tender. Rinse under cold water; drain.
3 Heat remaining oil in wok. Stir-fry onion and ginger until onion is soft; remove from wok. Stir-fry beef, in batches, until browned.
4 Return beef to wok. Add onion mixture, tomato and asparagus; stir-fry until heated through. Serve sprinkled with coriander and peanuts.

serves 4
preparation time 15 minutes (plus refrigeration time)
cooking time 15 minutes
per serving 19.3g total fat (5.2g saturated fat); 1388kJ (332 cal); 6.9g carbohydrate; 31.2g protein; 3.6g fibre

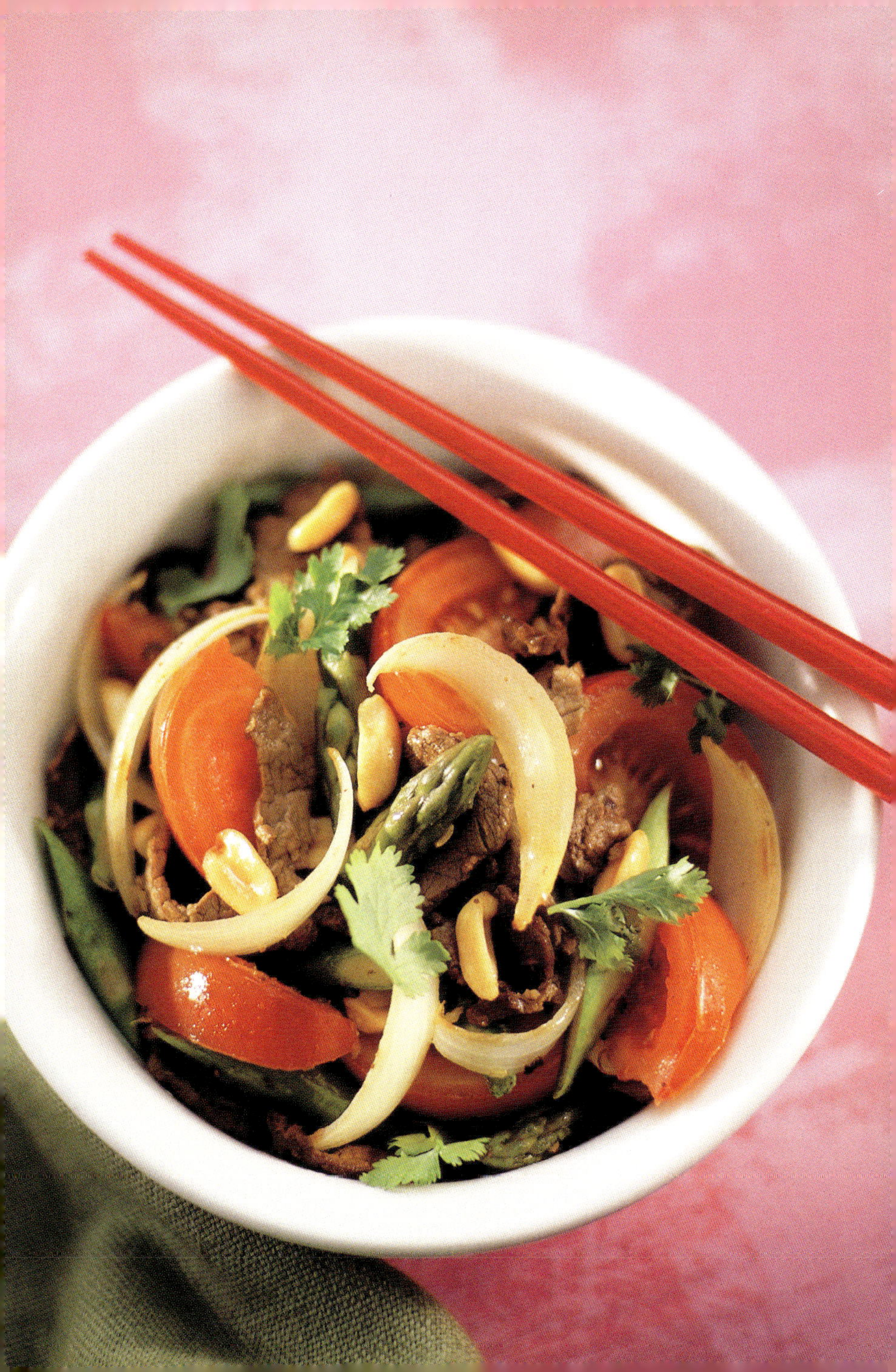

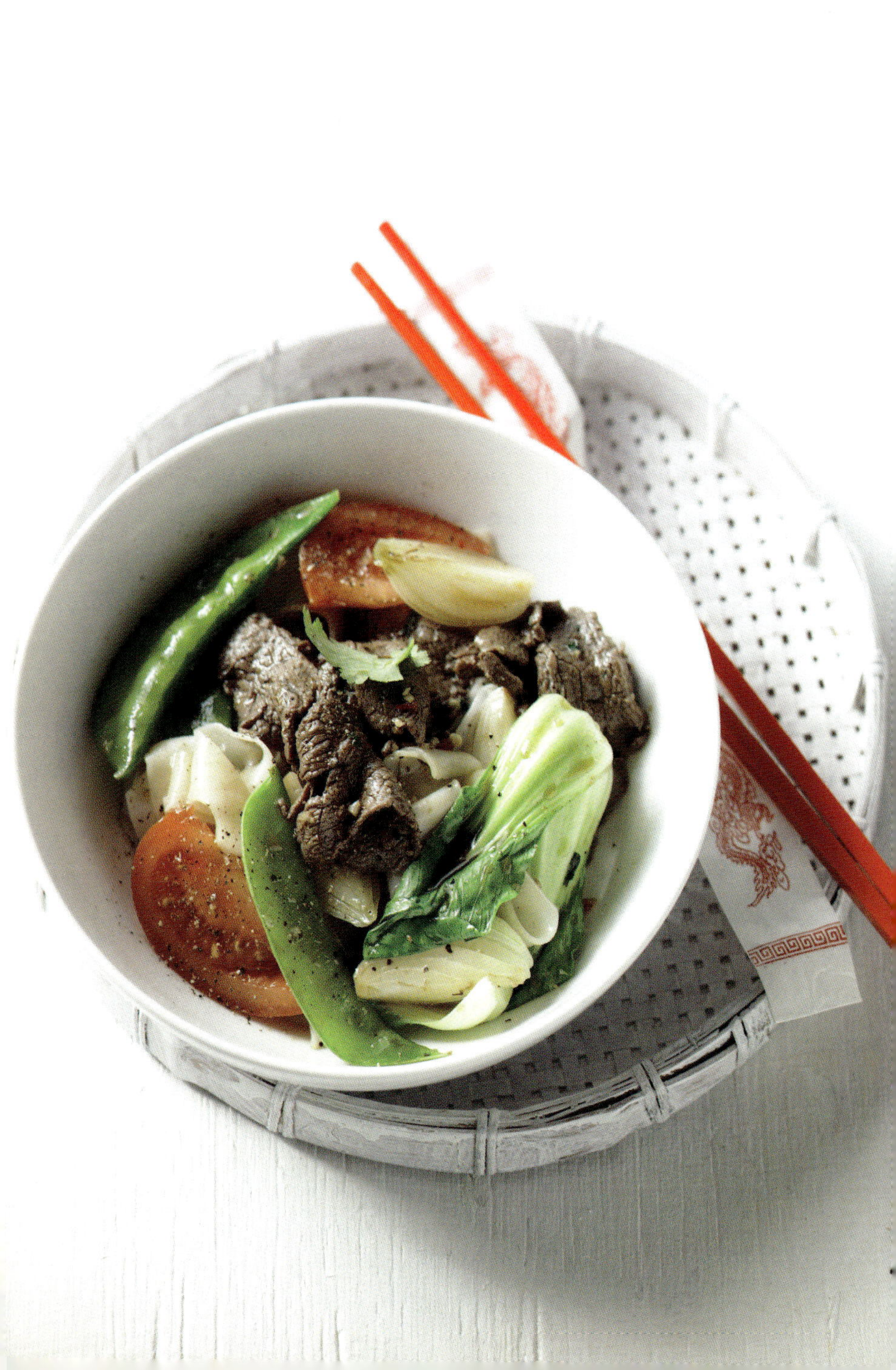

chilli beef and vegetables with noodles

500g piece beef fillet, thinly sliced
4 cloves garlic, crushed
¼ cup (60ml) fish sauce
1 tablespoon soy sauce
2 tablespoons oyster sauce
3 fresh small red thai chillies, chopped finely
2 teaspoons brown sugar
10cm stick fresh lemon grass (20g), chopped finely
¼ cup coarsely chopped fresh coriander
450g thick rice noodles
2 teaspoons peanut oil
6 spring onions (150g), trimmed, quartered
150g snow peas
340g baby buk choy, chopped coarsely
2 medium tomatoes (300g), cut into wedges

1 Combine beef, garlic, sauces, chilli, sugar, lemon grass and coriander in large bowl; mix well. Cover, refrigerate 3 hours or overnight.
2 Place noodles in medium heatproof bowl, cover with boiling water; stand until just tender, drain.
3 Heat oil in wok; stir-fry beef mixture, in batches, until browned all over. Add onions to wok; stir-fry until onions are browned lightly.
4 Add snow peas, buk choy, tomatoes, noodles and beef mixture to wok; cook, stirring, until heated through.
5 Serve sprinkled with extra fresh coriander leaves, if desired.

serves 4
preparation time 20 minutes (plus refrigeration time)
cooking time 15 minutes
per serving 10.9g total fat (3.6g saturated); 1626kJ (389 cal); 35.6g carbohydrate; 34.1g protein; 5.1g fibre
tip Scotch fillet, eye-fillet or rump steak can be used for this recipe.

stir-fry beef and noodle

750g piece beef rump, sliced thinly
¼ cup (60ml) fish sauce
⅓ cup (80ml) oyster sauce
⅓ cup (80ml) sweet chilli sauce
3 cloves garlic, crushed
500g hokkien noodles
2 tablespoons peanut oil
2 large brown onions (400g), sliced thinly
200g snow peas
1 cup (80g) bean sprouts
1 fresh long red chilli, sliced thinly

1 Place beef in large bowl with half the combined sauces and garlic. Cover; refrigerate 3 hours or overnight.
2 Place noodles in large heatproof bowl, cover with boiling water; separate noodles with fork, drain.
3 Heat half the oil in wok. Stir-fry beef mixture, in batches, until browned all over and almost cooked.
4 Heat remaining oil in wok; stir-fry onion until soft. Add snow peas and sprouts; stir-fry 1 minute. Return beef and noodles to wok with remaining combined sauces and garlic; stir-fry until hot. Serve sprinkled with chilli.

serves 4
preparation time 10 minutes (plus refrigeration time)
cooking time 15 minutes
per serving 21.6g total fat (6.5g saturated fat); 2541kJ (608 cal); 48.9g carbohydrate; 50.5g protein; 6.8g fibre

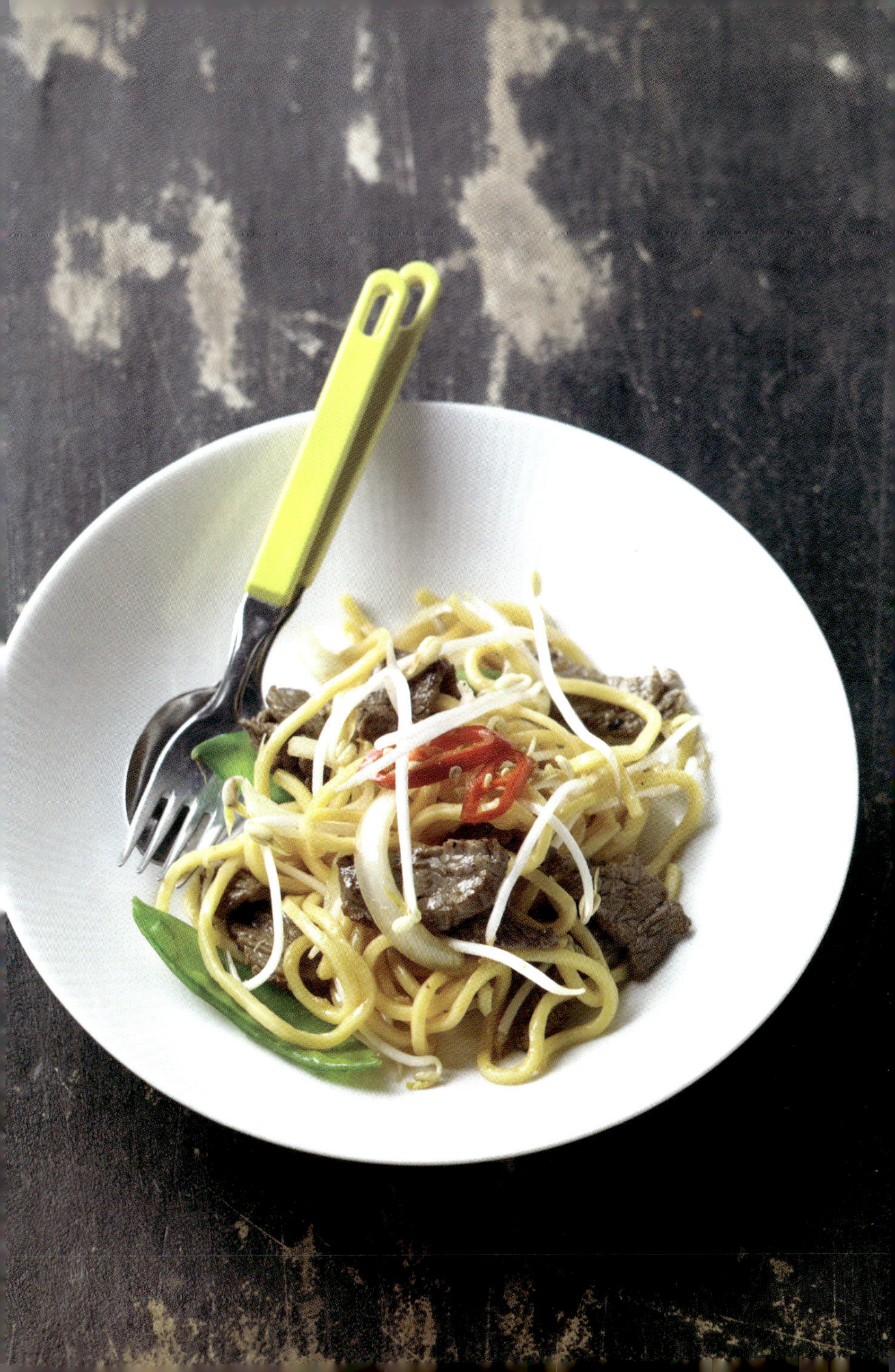

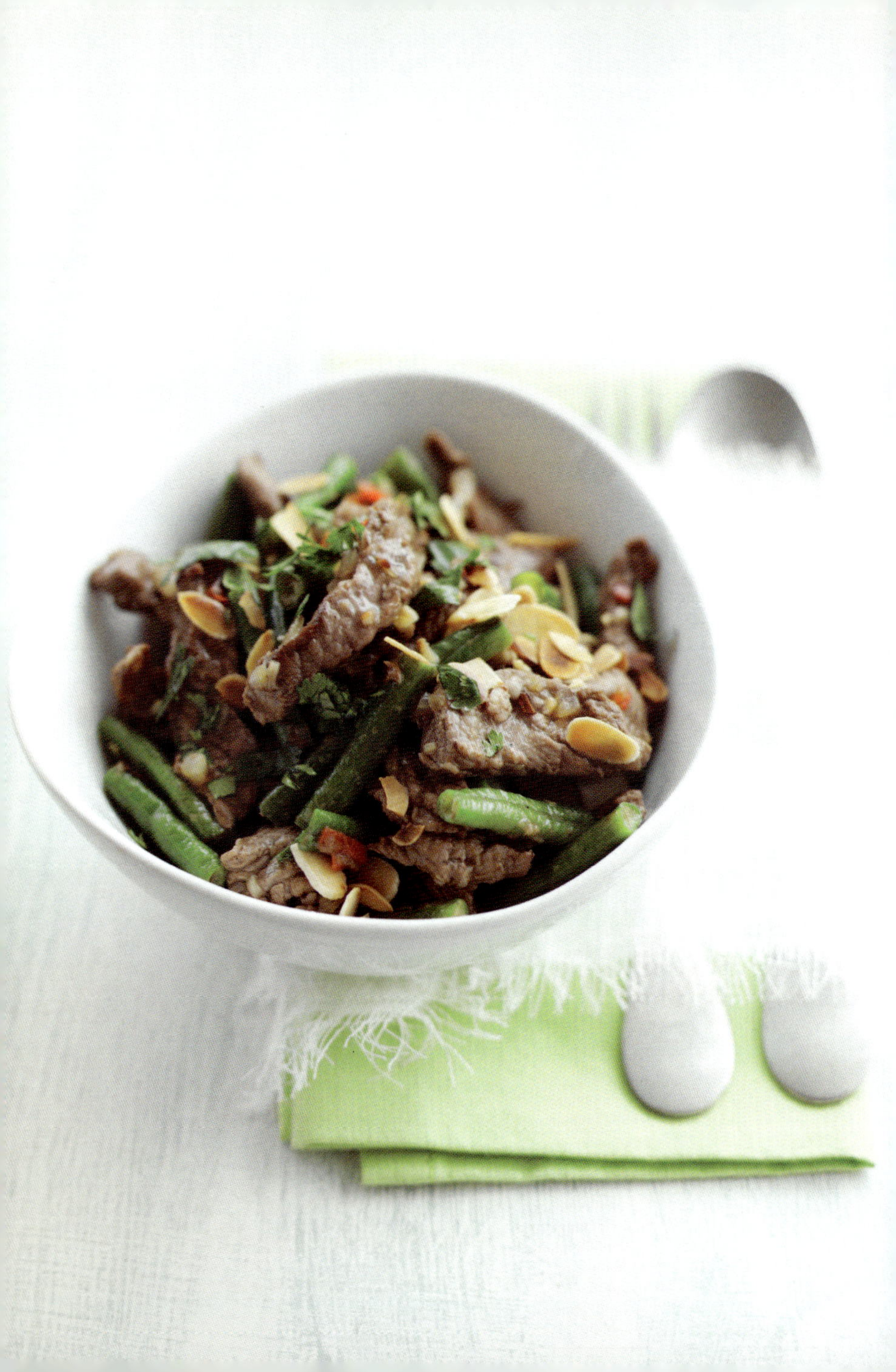

aromatic beef stirfry

2 tablespoons peanut oil
800g beef strips
1 medium brown onion (150g), chopped finely
3 cloves garlic, crushed
1 fresh long red chilli, chopped finely
10cm stick fresh lemon grass (20g), chopped finely
1 star anise
1 cinnamon stick
4 cardamom pods, bruised
350g snake beans, cut in 4cm lengths
2 tablespoons ground bean sauce
2 tablespoons fish sauce
½ cup coarsely chopped fresh coriander
½ cup (40g) roasted almond flakes

1 Heat half the oil in wok; stir-fry beef, in batches, until browned. Cover to keep warm.
2 Heat remaining oil in wok; stir-fry onion until soft. Add garlic, chilli, lemon grass, star anise, cinnamon, cardamom and beans; stir-fry until beans are tender. Discard star anise, cinnamon and cardamom.
3 Return beef to wok with sauces; stir-fry until heated through. Stir in coriander and nuts off the heat.

serves 4
preparation time 15 minutes
cooking time 15 minutes
per serving 27.2g total fat (7.2g saturated fat); 2002kJ (479 cal); 7.3g carbohydrate; 49.5g protein; 4.8g fibre
tips Ground bean sauce is a mixture of soy beans, flour, salt, sugar and water. To make your own version of ground bean sauce, add 1 teaspoon sugar to 1 tablespoon black bean sauce, if preferred.
Snake beans are long (about 40cm), thin, round, fresh green beans, Asian in origin, with a taste similar to green or french beans. They are also known as yard-long beans because of their (pre-metric) length.

chicken and tamarind stir-fry

2 cups (400g) jasmine rice
700g chicken breast fillets, sliced thinly
1 tablespoon tamarind concentrate
3 cloves garlic, crushed
2 fresh small red thai chillies, sliced thinly
2 teaspoons brown sugar
1 tablespoon lime juice
1 tablespoon peanut oil
1 large brown onion (200g), sliced thickly
½ cup loosely packed fresh coriander leaves

1 Cook rice in large saucepan of boiling water, uncovered, until just tender; drain.
2 Meanwhile, combine chicken, tamarind, garlic, chilli, sugar and juice in medium bowl.
3 Heat half the oil in wok; stir-fry chicken mixture, in batches, until browned all over and cooked through.
4 Heat remaining oil in wok; stir-fry onion until just softened. Return chicken to wok; toss gently to combine.
5 Serve chicken mixture with rice; sprinkle with coriander.

serves 4
preparation time 10 minutes
cooking time 15 minutes
per serving 9.2g total fat (2g saturated fat); 2579kJ (617 cal); 84.2g carbohydrate; 47.2g protein; 2.1g fibre

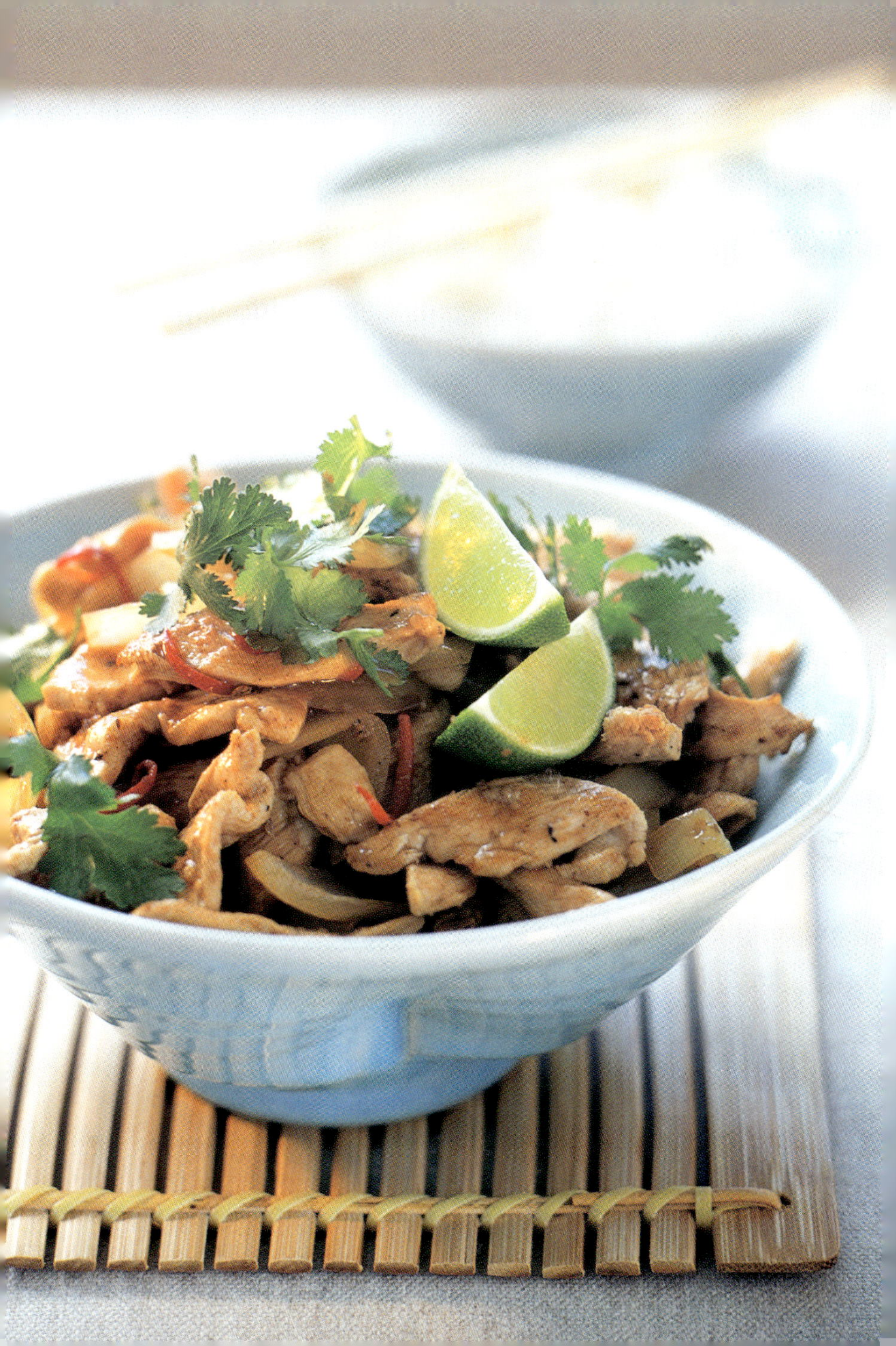

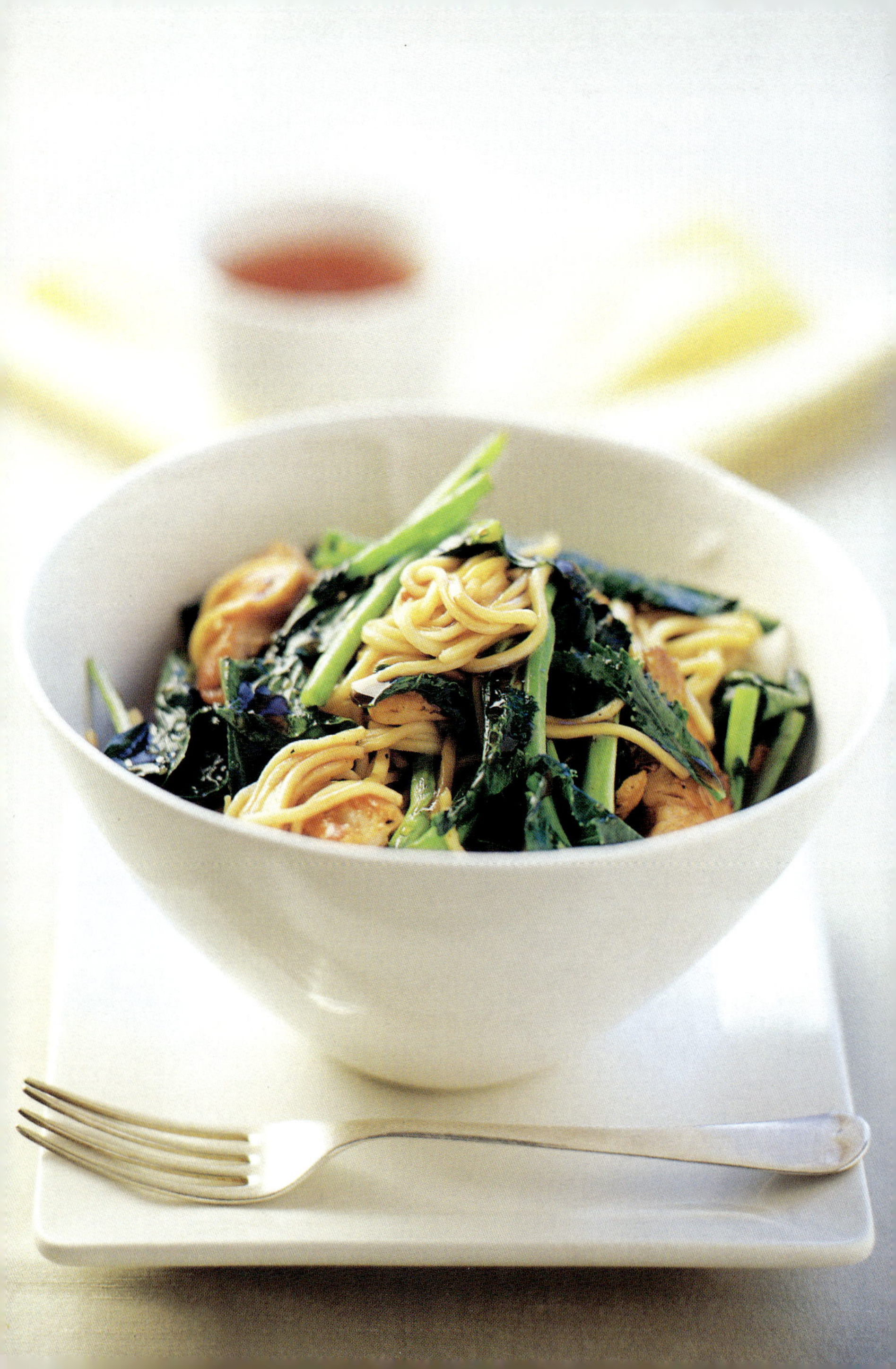

chicken and gai lan stir-fry

350g fresh singapore noodles
1 tablespoon peanut oil
750g chicken tenderloins, halved
1 large brown onion (200g), sliced thickly
3 cloves garlic, crushed
1kg gai lan, chopped coarsely
⅓ cup (80ml) oyster sauce
1 tablespoon light soy sauce

1 Place noodles in large heatproof bowl, cover with boiling water; separate noodles with fork, drain.
2 Heat half the oil in wok; stir-fry chicken, in batches, until browned all over and cooked through.
3 Heat remaining oil in wok; stir-fry onion and garlic until onion softens.
4 Return chicken to wok with gai lan and sauces; stir-fry until gai lan just wilts. Toss chicken mixture with noodles to serve.

serves 4
preparation time 10 minutes
cooking time 15 minutes
per serving 13.3g total fat (3.1g saturated fat); 1990kJ (476 cal); 32.5g carbohydrate; 50.1g protein; 11.9g fibre
tip Any type of fresh noodle can be used in this recipe.

sweet chilli dipping sauce

¼ cup (60ml) sweet chilli sauce
1 tablespoon lime juice
1 tablespoon fish sauce

1 Combine ingredients in small bowl.

makes ⅓ cup (80ml)
preparation time 5 minutes
per tablespoon 0.4g total fat
(0.1g saturated fat); 88kJ
(21 cal); 3.3g carbohydrate;
0.6g protein; 0.8g fibre

spicy dipping sauce

1 tablespoon rice vinegar
¼ cup (60ml) lime juice
1 clove garlic, crushed
1 tablespoon brown sugar
¼ cup (60ml) fish sauce
2 fresh small red thai chillies, sliced thinly
1 tablespoon finely chopped fresh coriander

1 Combine vinegar, juice, garlic, sugar and sauce in small jug; stand 15 minutes.
2 Strain sauce, discard garlic; stir in chilli and coriander.

makes ⅓ cup (80ml)
preparation time 10 minutes
(plus standing time)
per tablespoon 0.1g total fat
(0g saturated fat); 105kJ
(25 cal); 4.3g carbohydrate;
1.5g protein; 0.4g fibre

hoisin and peanut dipping sauce

2 teaspoons caster sugar
1 tablespoon rice vinegar
¼ cup (60ml) water
¼ cup (60ml) hoisin sauce
1 tablespoon crushed roasted peanuts

1 Combine sugar, vinegar and the water in small saucepan; stir over medium heat until sugar dissolves. Stir in sauce and nuts.

makes ⅔ cup (160ml)
preparation time 5 minutes
cooking time 2 minutes
per tablespoon 1.1g total fat (0.2g saturated fat); 125kJ (30 cal); 4.1g carbohydrate; 0.5g protein; 1g fibre

sweet and sour dipping sauce

¼ cup (60ml) white vinegar
½ cup (110g) caster sugar
1½ tablespoons water
¼ lebanese cucumber, seeded, chopped finely

1 Combine vinegar, sugar and the water in small saucepan; stir until sugar is dissolved. Boil, uncovered, 3 minutes, cool. Transfer to serving bowl; stir in cucumber.

makes ½ cup (125ml)
preparation time 5 minutes
cooking time 5 minutes
per tablespoon 0g total fat (0g saturated fat); 314kJ (75 cal); 18.4g carbohydrate; 0g protein; 0g fibre

conversion chart

MEASURES

One Australian metric measuring cup holds approximately 250ml, one Australian metric tablespoon holds 20ml, one Australian metric teaspoon holds 5ml.

The difference between one country's measuring cups and another's is within a 2- or 3-teaspoon variance, and will not affect your cooking results. North America, New Zealand and the United Kingdom use a 15ml tablespoon. All cup and spoon measurements are level. The most accurate way of measuring dry ingredients is to weigh them. When measuring liquids, use a clear glass or plastic jug with metric markings.

We use large eggs with an average weight of 60g.

DRY MEASURES

METRIC	IMPERIAL
15g	½oz
30g	1oz
60g	2oz
90g	3oz
125g	4oz (¼lb)
155g	5oz
185g	6oz
220g	7oz
250g	8oz (½lb)
280g	9oz
315g	10oz
345g	11oz
375g	12oz (¾lb)
410g	13oz
440g	14oz
470g	15oz
500g	16oz (1lb)
750g	24oz (1½lb)
1kg	32oz (2lb)

LIQUID MEASURES

METRIC	IMPERIAL
30ml	1 fluid oz
60ml	2 fluid oz
100ml	3 fluid oz
125ml	4 fluid oz
150ml	5 fluid oz (¼ pint/1 gill)
190ml	6 fluid oz
250ml	8 fluid oz
300ml	10 fluid oz (½ pint)
500ml	16 fluid oz
600ml	20 fluid oz (1 pint)
1000ml (1 litre)	1¾ pints

LENGTH MEASURES

METRIC	IMPERIAL
3mm	⅛in
6mm	¼in
1cm	½in
2cm	¾in
2.5cm	1in
5cm	2in
6cm	2½in
8cm	3in
10cm	4in
13cm	5in
15cm	6in
18cm	7in
20cm	8in
23cm	9in
25cm	10in
28cm	11in
30cm	12in (1ft)

OVEN TEMPERATURES

These oven temperatures are only a guide for conventional ovens. For fan-forced ovens, check the manufacturer's manual.

	°C (CELSIUS)	°F (FAHRENHEIT)	GAS MARK
Very slow	120	250	½
Slow	150	275 – 300	1 – 2
Moderately slow	160	325	3
Moderate	180	350 – 375	4 – 5
Moderately hot	200	400	6
Hot	220	425 – 450	7 – 8
Very hot	240	475	9

index

A
aromatic beef stir-fry 54
asparagus and
  lemon grass beef 49

B
barbecued chilli prawns with
  fresh mango salad 24
beef and rice noodle salad 39
beef stir-fry, aromatic 54
beef pho 4
beef, chilli, and vegetables
  with noodles 50
beef, lemon grass and
  asparagus 49
beef, stir-fry and noodle 53
buk choy with prawn
  tamarind stir-fry 44

C
caramel pork, spiced 47
chicken and gai lan stir-fry 58
chicken and tamarind stir-fry 57
chicken coconut
  summer rolls 19
chicken pho 7
chicken salad 27
chicken wonton soup 8
chicken wontons 8
chilli barbecued prawns with
  fresh mango salad 24
chilli beef and vegetables
  with noodles 50

D
dipping sauces
  hoisin and peanut 61
  spicy 60
  sweet and sour 61
  sweet chilli 60
dressings
  chicken salad 27
  duck salad 28
  ginger and lemon grass 31
  hot-smoked trout
    and vermicelli salad 32
  lime and chilli 39
  lime and garlic 35

prawn and vermicelli salad 36
duck and noodle salad 31
duck salad 28

M
mango salad, fresh 24

N
noodle and beef stir-fry 53
noodle and duck salad 31
noodle and vegetable
  summer rolls 20
noodle, rice, and beef salad 39
noodles with chilli beef
  and vegetables 50

O
omelettes, vegetable 40

P
pan-fried tofu with
  coleslaw salad 35
pho, beef 4
pho, chicken 7
pork and prawn summer rolls 23
pork, spiced caramel 47
prawn and pork summer rolls 23
prawn and vermicelli salad 36
prawn soup 11
prawn tamarind stir-fry
  with buk choy 44
prawns, barbecued chilli, with
  fresh mango salad 24

R
rice noodle and beef salad 39
rolls
  coconut chicken summer 19
  noodle and vegetable
    summer 20
  pork and prawn summer 23
  spring 16

S
salads
  beef and rice noodle 39
  chicken 27
  duck 28
  duck and noodle 31
  fresh mango 24

hot-smoked trout and
  vermicelli 32
pan-fried tofu with coleslaw 35
prawn and vermicelli 36
salt and lemon-pepper squid 15
sauces
  hoisin and peanut dipping 61
  spicy dipping 60
  sweet and sour dipping 61
  sweet chilli dipping 60
scallops, steamed sesame 12
sesame scallops, steamed 12
soup, chicken wonton 8
soup, prawn 11
spiced caramel pork 47
spicy dipping sauce 60
spring rolls 16
squid, salt and
  lemon-pepper 15
steamed sesame scallops 12
stir-fried mixed vegetables 43
stir-fry
  aromatic beef 54
  beef and noodle 53
  chicken and gai lan 58
  chicken and tamarind 57
  prawn tamarind with
    buk choy 44

T
tamarind and chicken stir-fry 57
tofu, pan-fried, with
  coleslaw salad 35
trout, hot-smoked, and
  vermicelli salad 32

V
vegetable and noodle
  summer rolls 20
vegetable omelettes 40
vegetables and chilli beef
  with noodles 50
vegetables, stir-fried mixed 43
vermicelli and hot-smoked
  trout salad 32
vermicelli and prawn salad 36

W
wontons, chicken 8

63

Are you missing some of the world's favourite cookbooks?

The Australian Women's Weekly cookbooks are available from bookshops, cookshops, supermarkets and other stores all over the world. You can also buy direct from the publisher, using the order form below.

MINI SERIES £3.50 190x138MM 64 PAGES

TITLE	QTY	TITLE	QTY	TITLE	QTY
4 Fast Ingredients		Fast Food for Friends		Potatoes	
15-minute Feasts		Fast Soup		Risotto	
50 Fast Chicken Fillets		Finger Food		Roast	
50 Fast Desserts		Gluten-free Cooking		Salads	
After-work Stir-fries		Healthy Everyday Food 4 Kids		Simple Slices	
Barbecue		Ice-creams & Sorbets		Simply Seafood	
Barbecue Chicken		Indian Cooking		Skinny Food	
Barbecued Seafood		Indonesian Favourites		Spanish Favourites	
Biscuits, Brownies & Biscotti		Italian Favourites		Stir-fries	
Bites		Jams & Jellies		Summer Salads	
Bowl Food		Japanese Favourites		Tapas, Antipasto & Mezze	
Burgers, Rösti & Fritters		Kids Party Food		Thai Cooking	
Cafe Cakes		Last-minute Meals		Thai Favourites	
Cafe Food		Lebanese Cooking		The Fast Egg	
Casseroles		Low-Fat Delicious		The Packed Lunch	
Char-grills & Barbecues		Low Fat Fast		Vegetarian	
Cheesecakes, Pavlova & Trifles		Malaysian Favourites		Vegetarian Stir-fries	
Chinese Favourites		Mince		Vegie Main Meals	
Chocolate Cakes		Mince Favourites		Vietnamese Favourites	
Christmas Cakes & Puddings		Muffins		Wok	
Cocktails		Noodles		Young Chef	
Crumbles & Bakes		Outdoor Eating			
Curries		Party Food			
Dried Fruit & Nuts		Pasta			
Drinks		Pickles and Chutneys		TOTAL COST	£

Photocopy and complete coupon below

ACP Magazines Ltd Privacy Notice
This book may contain offers, competitions or surveys that require you to provide information about yourself if you choose to enter or take part in any such Reader Offer.
If you provide information about yourself to ACP Magazines Ltd, the company will use this information to provide you with the products or services you have requested, and may supply your information to contractors that help ACP to do this. ACP will also use your information to inform you of other ACP publications, products, services and events. ACP will also give your information to organisations that are providing special prizes or offers, and that are clearly associated with the Reader Offer.
Unless you tell us not to, we may give your information to other organisations that use it to inform you about other products, services and events or who may give it to other organisations that may use it for this purpose. If you would like to gain access to the information ACP holds about you, please contact ACP's Privacy Officer at:
ACP Magazines Ltd, 54-58 Park Street, Sydney, NSW 2000, Australia

☐ Privacy Notice: Please do not provide information about me to any organisation not associated with this offer.

Name _____
Address _____
_____ Postcode _____
Country _____ Phone (business hours) _____
Email*(optional) _____
* By including your email address, you consent to receipt of any email regarding this magazine, and other emails which inform you of ACP's other publications, products, services and events, and to promote third party goods and services you may be interested in.

I enclose my cheque/money order for £ _____ or please charge £ _____
to my: ☐ Access ☐ Mastercard ☐ Visa ☐ Diners Club
PLEASE NOTE: WE DO NOT ACCEPT SWITCH OR ELECTRON CARDS

Card number | | | | | | | | | | | | | | | |

3 digit security code *(found on reverse of card)* _____

Cardholder's
signature _____ Expiry date ___/___

To order: Mail or fax – photocopy or complete the order form above, and send your credit card details or cheque payable to: Australian Consolidated Press (UK), Moulton Park Business Centre, Red House Road, Moulton Park, Northampton NN3 6AQ, phone (+44) (0) 1 604 497533, fax (+44) (0) 1 604 497533, e-mail books@acpuk.com. Or order online at www.acpuk.com
Non-UK residents: We accept the credit cards listed on the coupon, or cheques, drafts or International Money Orders payable in sterling and drawn on a UK bank. Credit card charges are at the exchange rate current at the time of payment.
All pricing current at time of going to press and subject to change/availability.
Postage and packing UK: Add £1.00 per order plus 25p per book.
Postage and packing overseas: Add £2.00 per order plus 50p per book. **Offer ends 31.12.2007**